© 2007 Shadress Denise
© 2007 Blue Indigo Publishing

ISBN-13: 978-0-9981484-1-0

Publisher | Blue Indigo Publishing
Book Cover Designer | ColorMeBlu Designs www.colormebludesigns.com
Interior Design | Strawberry Publications, LLC
www.StrawberryPublications.com

All rights reserved. This book contains material protected under International and Federal Copyright Laws and Treaties. Any unauthorized reprint or use of this material is prohibited. No part of this book may be reproduced or transmitted in any form or by any means, electronic or mechanical, including photocopying, recording or by any information storage and retrieval system without express writer permission from the author/publisher.

This is a work of fiction. Any references or similarities to actual events, real people, living or dead, or to the real locals are intended to give the novel a sense of reality. Any similarity in other names, characters, places, and incidents are entirely coincidental.

Also written by Shadress Denise

Disturbia
Who Do You Love?
Who Do You Love Too?
hello. goodbye. never again

LIBERATION

You've laid dormant for so long and
now the door has been opened.
You walked through
and now everything seems so much clearer.

You showed me a person I never knew existed.
I am free when I feel you near.

Every time my pen touches a piece of paper, your
presence comes alive.
Thank you for being my strength and my voice. My
reason to finally be strong and move on.

You liberated me and now I am free.

SHADRESS

TABLE OF CONTENTS

INDECENT PROPOSAL
NEVER SAY NEVER
HIDDEN MONSTER
ROADBLOCKS
TEMPORARY
SUPERMAN
SUGAR WALLS
ZODIAC
THE ZONE
THE ONE
BEHIND CLOSED DOORS
G-SPOT
QUIETLY SCREAMING
HEADACHE
POSITIONS
SEDUCTIVE CHASE
INVASION
SEXUAL STIMULATION
SIDE PIECE
SINFUL DANCE
THE MADFUCKER
MIRROR
LOOSE ENDS
MEMORY BANK
STRUNG OUT
HIS MISTRESS
DADDY'S MISTAKE
MIDNIGHT HOUR
JUST PASSING
CHEATERS
LOVE'S CRIME
STOPLIGHT
SONGBIRD
PILLOW TALK
UNSTABLE
DISTRACTION
SHADOW DANCE
MIND SEX
HIS WORLD

TABLE OF CONTENTS

SUBMISSIVE
THE ARTIST
RAINSHOWER
INSANITY
PEEP SHOW
SELFISH
CORRUPT
THE PRICE OF FREEDOM
POETRY TO ME
BAGGAGE
ABANDONED
ESCAPE
FORGIVENESS
PAIN RELIEVER
DESIRES
CONVERSATION
STOLEN MOMENTS
SURREAL
REBIRTH
COLD TURKEY
UPSIDE DOWN
DREAMCHASER
FREEDOM DANCE
DOSAGE
NO SUBSTITUTION
FIRESTARTER
UNDERESTIMATED
ACCEPTANCE
POSSESSED
ILLUSIONS
BEDTIME SECRETS
TWISTED
CONSUMPTION
OVERDOSE
REPLACED
ARRIVED
SCENT
SEXUALLY UNLEASED
VACANT

TABLE OF CONTENTS

CLOSURE
LISTEN
INDENTITY CRISIS
LIBERATED
STRIPPED
TRICKED
TURNED OUT
RECOVERED
THE LAST TIME
JUDGMENT
DEATH SENTENCE
LOVE'S FATALITY
DEVIL'S KITCHEN
SET-UP
HEALING
CIVILIZED EVIL
BLIND SENSES
CONFESSIONS
SILENCED PLEA
IMPERFECTIONS
BRICK WALL

LIBERATED

INDECENT PROPOSAL

He walks pass me
and I feel the tension.
His eyes are filled
with lust as he stares at me.
I feel him behind me
as his breath makes
my skin turn tricks.
He sends a tingle
down my spine as
his fingers caress my back.
He walks away with a
smile on his face;
a signal he gives as he
commands me to follow him
to our secret place. He
buries his face within my
walls and he goes
where no man has ever gone before.
Our hidden spot,
tucked away for
our indecent proposals.

SHADRESS DENISE

NEVER SAY NEVER

Never again will I hurt you.
Words that play in my
head over and over again,
from this person I thought was my man.

Never again will I hit you.
Sincere words I thought were true
as I stand in front of my mirror,
packing makeup on the rings around
my eyes that are now black and blue.

Never again will I flaunt
another woman in your face.
Apologies I accepted once again,
as I see her walking out of my place.

Never again will I be free.
Words that are now my reality,
as I pull the trigger and
you fall to your knees.

LIBERATED

HIDDEN MONSTER

You created her, so
she's all yours.
Night after night, I
sat up crying,
waiting and pissed off
while you were out with
your whores.
You never knew how
to treat me.
You've taken advantage
of my feelings,
abusing my kindness for
weakness.
You promised you were leaving,
yet you are still creating drama
for me.

My heart has fallen apart,
due to bad intentions
you had from the start.
You say mad is what
I make you and there are
so many things she is
I will never be.
You don't like what you see
and you are ready to leave,
but you can't go anywhere darling
until we deal with this

SHADRESS DENISE

monster you've created within me.

LIBERATED

ROADBLOCKS

Shadows standing in the distance,
but I feel your presence is near.
The constant knocking of failure and
the sudden rise of fear.
A sure step of commitment I
decide to take.
As you move closer to
sit and wait patiently
for me to fall and completely break.

TEMPORARY

You wonder where you stand
with the person you call your man.
You need to know if this will last
because he says he
loves you and you are not
just some piece of ass.
You hold him tight
while you make love all night.
He calls her name
and all you feel is shame.
You gave it up so
fast there's no way he's to
blame.

LIBERATED

SUPERMAN

slowly removing my clothes as I move
under you ready for you to
position yourself on top of me.
eager and excited while I lay here
ready to feel you inside me.
making me moan
as you slide in and out, giving me
never ending orgasms I've waited so long to feel.

Sugar Walls

He enters me and my
juices become a connection
between me and him.
He gently glides
in and out as I moan
with great pleasure.
He is butter and I am brown sugar,
he takes me to new heights
and I begin to give in.
I reach the top
and my guard falls.
I lay still as
the sweet mixture
of a beautiful
moment
flows from my sugar walls.

LIBERATED

ZODIAC

I don't know where he came from,
but he's here to stay.
The moment our souls met,
I knew no other man
could make me feel this way.
I feel his hands caress and glide
over every inch of me.
He makes me feel sexy, wanted,
and so fulfilled.
I can't explain
why I love him so much,
but when I am near him,
there is no place I want to go but up.

We have such an unbelievable
cosmic connection,
it sometimes seems unreal.
The ying to my yang,
he feels what I feel.
My orgasm mounts and
my soul cries out,
leaving me to feel
like I'm in place I've never seen.
I smile knowing I
have a lifetime to spend reaching
for the stars with this freaky,
sensitive, amazing man who came to
me from afar.

SHADRESS DENISE

THE ZONE

Once you enter,
there is no turning back.
A world that is constantly spinning,
ecstasy grabs hold and takes
control.
It leaves you yearning for more,
giving you such a spectacular
after, you won't remember the before.
You become greedy and unable to stop.
Your body is set on fire,
and so much tension begins to build up.
You want to escape and you crave to be released.
You try to escape by departing,
but the zone is not ready for you to leave.
You scream as your body is turned inside out,
you beg for mercy as your body
begins to explode from the orgasm
the zone finally allows you to mount.

LIBERATED

THE ONE

Who is the one or how do you
know if you are the one?
A confusing, yet a desired feeling a
woman dreams of having
while sometimes creating and giving
this title to the wrong man.

How do you know if you are the one?
Is it a destined feeling you are born with
that connects you to someone else,
or is it a special bond you form
when you meet someone along the way?
Does it start with the way your mate approaches you, or
that first smile or that first glance
you make from across the room?

How do you know your true love
lies within this person?
Do you create an imaginary future
before the first conversation?
or do you plan the rest of your life
after your first date?

What makes him the one?
Is it how he takes his time to
inquire about your mental,
emotional, and spiritual status, or
is the way he curls your feet
while he rushes to get you between the sheets?

Is it how he's not drawn to everything
he sees or is it an illusion you are
trapped in when you tell yourself he's only with me.

SHADRESS DENISE

A belief that keeps you sane as he walks in late,
continuously lying while creating the numb feeling
you've developed to block out the pain.

He loves me,
a lie you play over and over in
your head while he moves
in and out some other woman's bed.

He screams it's not true
while you block his fists from hitting you again,
leaving rings around your eyes that you know will
eventually turn black and blue.
You tell your friends they don't have a clue
while you convince yourself this will last,
because he loves you and only you.

Foolish girl you cry at night
all the while you see the end is near. He
sheds his tears telling you a life
without you is his biggest fear.
You pull him close as you listen to
the apologies all the
while your spirit yearns to be free.
You allow his fingers run up and down your spine, too
naive to realize that once again
he has taken over your mind.
Your heart screams out with rage,
but you can't walk away because
he is what you want and what you crave.

The quick fix you get from the dick
you know will soon be in and out of some other bitch. You
yell out you are tired of this shit,
mad at the fact your heart
doesn't know when to quit.
Still you believe the lie
that one day you'll be his wife.

LIBERATED

You pack your bags and you head for the door,
while he crawls on his knees promising
he is finish and he won't do it anymore.
You yell whatever and beg him to stop,
while you see him reach
in his pocket and pull out a box.
He stands to his feet knowing
a little bling from a diamond ring
placed on your finger is what you
need to make sure he won't linger.

You fall for the trap so he knows
it's a wrap, no more questions
while he's out looking for
the next piece of ass to tap.

The wakeup call comes when you lay in
bed upset and crying.
He's back to his old ways you believed
he would stop because he bought you a diamond ring.

The day comes and you realize
the drama this man brings.
You refuse to be a woman
trapped by a little bling.
You stand to your feet grabbing the bags
you once left at the door walking out convinced
that the bullshit is unnecessary
and you aren't taking it anymore.
No longer caring about being the one.

SHADRESS DENISE

BEHIND CLOSED DOORS

If these walls could talk,
oh the stories they would tell.
They would whisper the things
you do to make
my heart melt.
If these walls had eyes,
they could see the way you
caress my body and make my
temperature rise. If these
walls had ears, they could
hear the moans of ecstasy,
as we let our inhibitions
run wild,
free from any fear.
If these walls had arms,
they would you pull you
close and make you
feel things you've never
felt before.
Creating a safe haven
for our secrets,
that will always remain
behind closed doors.

LIBERATED

G-SPOT

I wait anxiously for you
to arrive at the place
you so desperately want to be.
A quick burst
of passion ignites a fire
that burns throughout me.
I am a prisoner
waiting for you
to unlock the door
and set me free.
Ready to run
to a place that blows
my mind as you enter me
from behind.
I realize why I love
to feel you
close and never
want you to stop.
You control
my every move as
you hit my spot.

QUIETLY SCREAMING

I try and block out the
pain by not bringing up her name.
I reminisce about good times, but it
seems like nothing
will ever be the same.
You gave away our love and
it doesn't seem fair.
You fucked her without guilt,
because you never really cared.
My hands want to shake,
but I won't let them move.
The tears want to fall
so I wipe them away.
The memories start to escape
and I can't stop them.
Some days' history is quiet, but
today it screams out loud.

LIBERATED

HEADACHE

I've sat and I've waited,
and today I am leaving.
Yesterday's burdens will
only be false promises
of tomorrow because you
lied and you cheated.
You say you don't
know what for,
but the truth is you're full of
shit and very immature.
My strength has faded
and there's nothing left to give.
I cannot take the pain and
the tainted memories have
taken over my brain. There
is no use in trying to
repair a love that doesn't
exist and is
no longer the same.

… SHADRESS DENISE

POSITIONS

Variations of our
lovemaking as we
experience and create
so many new things.

SEDUCTIVE CHASE

The lust in your eyes
draws me in closer as I
imagine your hands
caressing my skin.
I squeeze tight
as the throbbing feeling
yearns for me to give in.
My mind is screaming for
me to stop,
while my body is begging
for more.
I feel the tension intensifying
as I turn to walk out the door.

INVASION

The thoughts that were once mine, now
belong to him.
The smile that glides across my face,
comes only when I think about him.
The sound of his name
removes all of my pain and
leaves me to wonder where
would I be without him.
I am a hostage,
my heart has been captured.
I was once a rebel,
now I surrender to love.

LIBERATED

SEXUAL STIMULATION

I sit and think about all the ways
we are breaking the rules.
Playing with a fire
we both love to ignite.
Constantly walking in
a zone that is dangerous. We
approach our situation we
know is both erotic
and rebellious with no caution.
I sit and watch you hold her hand,
pulling her close,
pretending to be her man.

SHADRESS DENISE

SIDE PIECE

I'm never going
to be his lady
because I'm hidden
behind closed doors.
Heartbroken and sore
from being his whore.
He tells me in the future there
will be more,
but at this time he is torn.
I believe one day
he's gonna get his shit and go, but
it won't be with me because I
allowed him
to treat me like a hoe.

SINFUL DANCE

I watch as your leg twirls
with such grace.
The temptation in your
eyes exude this exotic
look from your face.
The dance that you
do continues to reel me in.
I melt at the thought of
how your touch makes me feel.
Your moves send jolts
of heat throughout my skin,
while my body continues to
fight a battle you are determined to win.
Your lips on my body,
gives me such a rush,
through the harmonious rhythm
we create as our bodies touch.
The dance you do always pulls me in, as
the night causes me to forget about her
and give in to our most unforgivable
sins.

SHADRESS DENISE

THE MAD FUCKER

He comes to me
in the middle of the night.
Never am I worried or disappointed
because he always does it right.
He never talks about turning me out.
He handles his business
by showing me what fucking is all about.
As the nectar runs down my thigh, the
aroma of sex is making me high.
The heat in the room
leaves me hot,
as he moves his tongue in and out,
constantly hitting my spot.
To him pleasing me is not a game, satisfaction
comes to him when I scream his name.
He knows I have to have it each and every
night, so he makes sure he's on point when
it comes to fucking me right.

LIBERATED

MIRROR

It watches us as
we hold each other close.
It sees the looks you
make as I massage
your skin and kiss your spot.
It holds the steam in the
room as the intensity we
create begins to
make things hot.
The reflections we see
are of pure satisfaction. I
see you and you see me,
we gaze into each other's eyes,
while the mirror shows
our entire night of ecstasy.

LOOSE ENDS

I thought what we shared was over.
The look in your eyes
and the smile on my face,
tell all of the
connection we thought
was lost.
A glimpse into your eyes,
draws me back in.
The anger I once
had towards you,
no longer lies
within. Just to be near you
sends an all too familiar
feeling throughout my body.
Breaking me down to the
very element in which I began,
as it lets
me know this will never be
over.
The beginning to a game
we are not ready to end.

LIBERATED

MEMORY BANK

You are the first
thing on my mind
when I wake up.
A feeling of anxiousness
comes over me and
sometimes I wonder
will I get to see you today?
I dial your number
just to hear your voice.
I look at your
picture just to see your
smile. In my mind I create
excuses to see your face,
to smell your scent,
and to feel your touch.
I daydream about the
way you hold me.
Fantasize about the
way you make love to me.
I yearn for that
daily exotic thought I keep
stored inside forever.

SHADRESS DENISE

Strung Out

Like a hunter who
searches for his next victim,
you've captured me.
The way you make love to me,
places me under this hypnotic
spell that devours and
controls me.
Like a fiend that craves
her regular fix,
I need you.
The constant mind blowing
sex is like overdosed
injections of you that makes
me climb walls
and hang from a high that
melts my heart and calms my soul.
You drive me to an
euphoric level,
creating   illusions
that blow my mind.
I am your junkie,
and you are my pusher.
A fiend left in a world
of ecstasy that has me
strung out.

LIBERATED

HIS MISTRESS

She stares at me with
this oh so familiar face.
I've seen her before.
Somehow I can't remember where as
the awkward vibe
she gives is so out of place.
A feeling of betrayal
consumes me and this uneasiness
I can't seem to shake.
As she walks by, her
facial features are
forever implanted in my head.
The scent she is
wearing reminds me of
something I have
smelled in my bed.

DADDY'S MISTAKE

You told me you wanted me for life, as
I took your ring and
said yes to being your wife.
I lay in this bed and
all I do is cry to
your bullshit stories that
end up being lies.
You say you love me,
but I don't understand why
you continue to play these
games and you say you're a man.
Night after night,
and fight after fight, I
stand by you, knowing
people are
talking about me being a damn fool.
Now here you stand
with something we
should have shared.
Proof you thought with your dick,
letting me know you didn't care.
A child that isn't ours,
but yet yours.
A child not created with your wife,
the lasting memory of your whore.

LIBERATED

MIDNIGHT HOUR

When it comes around,
I know you're not far behind.
I lie here naked.
Patiently waiting for your
arrival, your touch, and
your kisses that send
electric sensations
throughout my body.
As I lay on my back, I
feel the warmth of
your body
as you enter me
with such passion,
creating the sweat that
falls from your face.
Teardrops of sex that
show the intensity
of what we do when
you invade my space.

SHADRESS DENISE

Just Passing

It's a beautiful day
and I see you.
We walk by each other and
I feel the chemistry that
was once there.
I speak and all of
the memories begin to
play back in my mind.
You say "hello" and ask
how have I been?

I smile,
wanting at that very moment
to tell you how much
I've missed you.
We hug and our eyes lock, confirming
each other's thoughts. I invite you to
my place,
and you accept wanting to
feel me near you just once more. We
spend an entire afternoon getting
reacquainted
as we make love,
holding each other close.

You tell me everything I
want to hear and I listen,
knowing this was a once

LIBERATED

in a lifetime moment.
I smile as I move closer,
laughing at the notion
of what happens from just passing by.

SHADRESS DENISE

CHEATERS

Gambling
with the game of love.
Taking shortcuts on the path
that leads to our hearts.
Creating risks that
will end up deadly.
Lying here with you
knowing I have to go
home to him.

LIBERATED

LOVE'S CRIME

I lie here on the ground,
numb from the pain
that has yet to kick in. I
turn my head,
to see the pool of blood
my body has created.
I look to see you standing over me,
pointing a gun while you continue to
yell at the man that is
lying at my side.
The dizziness begins to wear off, as
I feel the pain from where
the bullet went in.
You bend down
to kiss me and to say goodbye. I
begin to realize all the drama I
created from a lie.
My eyes begin to close and

I hear you whisper,
"to have and to hold,
until death do us part."

All the misery I created
from playing with your heart.

STOPLIGHT

I turned to look at you,
watching you as you
patiently wait for it to turn.
Just sitting here,
makes me realize how
much I want you.
I've always fantasized about
doing something crazy
and spontaneous with you.
I fix it so we can't move,
while I crawl and mount
myself on top of you.
We slowly move to each
other's rhythm as time
seems to stop.
I feel myself explode,
as the noise from around
us begins to become a distraction.
We laugh as we fix
ourselves to move,
excited to make it
to our next stop.

LIBERATED

SONGBIRD

I take my seat
just in time
to see the spotlight shine
on your silhouette, hidden
by the darkness on the
stage.

I sit and listen to you sing,
while I am completely
mesmerized by your strong,
yet sexy voice.
I watch you closely
as your body sways to the music.

My adrenaline immediately
moves faster as I watch
your lips cover the microphone,
while your voice begins to rise.
I become wrapped up in your aura, as
your hands glide up
and down the pole.

Our eyes meet and I feel the control I
walked in with,
slipping away.

Your gaze so exotic,
your moves so erotic,
as you continued to
draw me in with your

melody of temptation.

LIBERATED

PILLOW TALK

I lay awake as I
listen to the
things you whisper in my ear.
A sound that creates this
pleasurable explosion
between my legs.

UNSTABLE

I can't fight the feeling,
because it's so incredibly
appealing.
There's something about
it, that makes me doubt it.
I can't resist the craves,
that push me to the
edge of rage.
It is something I can't see,
but feel reaching out for me.
Begging for the excitement,
the desire to be free.
The need to be wanted,
the high it takes you on
once it has been released.

DISTRACTION

He's sitting next to me
as I pick up the phone
to tell you wrong number.
I say goodbye
but you ask me to wait.
You tell me you know he's there,
but you really don't care.
You called to hear my voice,
but now that's not enough.
You want me to cum
before you hang up.
I tell you that's not
possible and you say walk away. I
begin to move,
but stop worried about
what he might say.
You tell me that you're
naked and I hear you moan,
as I sit there silently screaming,
wishing this was just a dream.
The remnants of pleasure
glides down
my leg as I beg you to stop,
telling you this so wrong.
You laugh and I smile, truly
satisfied from
the pleasure I received
from the other end of the phone.

SHADRESS DENISE

SHADOW DANCE

I gaze at the wall and begin to
see a playback of
what happened a few hours before.
I moan as I focus my eyes on
the way he touches her,
reminding me of how you touch me.

I watch as he takes his
hand and traces her silhouette
with a smile of appreciation.
She pulls him close,
only to kiss him with such passion.
She feels his temperature rising,
letting her know he's ready
to create something new.
She spreads her legs
to invite him into her world
of ecstasy.
I see how her body
constantly yearns for him.
Her legs lock together,
rolling him over as she
mounts him with complete control.

He grips her hips,
as she moves to the beat
he knows so well.
Their bodies begin to shake,

LIBERATED

as their souls fall over the
edge of pleasure.

He reaches for her to come close,
and she slowly collapses, giving
him the satisfaction
I give you when our bodies
have finished our dance.

SHADRESS DENISE

MIND SEX

I see him and he sees me.
We smile at each other,
acknowledging one another's thoughts.
He walks to a corner,
never breaking the eye contact we
have established.
I continue to stare at him
as he mentally stimulates my mind,
distracting me from the
throbbing feeling between my thighs.
I undress him with my eyes,
as I see him standing in front of me.
Holding himself as he patiently waits
for me to devour him.
I open my mouth,
inviting him in so I
can taste the sweetness of him.
I move back and forth,
as he grabs my head,
letting me know the intensity of
the pleasure he is receiving.
I hold him close as I feel him explode,
letting me know he has been satisfied.
I swallow my dose of ecstasy,
as I give him one last lick.
I hear my name being called next,
I smile letting him know how
much I enjoyed our game of mind sex.

LIBERATED

HIS WORLD

I am so wrapped up,
I can't explain how.
I am in a world
beyond my control.
I stand here paralyzed, as
he holds her hand and
walks right past me.
My insides feel so heavy
and my knees are so weak.
My mind is racing from
all the things I've just seen.
I remember how just yesterday
he said it was all about me.
Promises of how I am enough woman
for him and how there will
never be any reason for him to cheat.
I am so wrapped up,
I can't begin to explain,
how I'm stuck in a world
where I am one of his many girls.

Submissive

I give him my heart as
he holds my hands,
and takes control.
I allow him to have
his way with me,
while he gives me
a desirable amount of pleasure.
I lie still as he captures
the essence of what it means
to make love to a woman.
He finishes and I pause,
paralyzed and hypnotized
with the things he has done to me. I
open my eyes as he turns me over.
My insides smile,
ready to endure whatever he has next.

LIBERATED

THE ARTIST

Standing here,
I smile as I look
upon this re-creation of me.
I gaze upon the
precise way you beautifully
captured the very
crux of my shape.
I sit and listen to the
melody that breezes
through my ears
and comes from your heart.
As the poetic
lyrics flow from
your lips,
I begin to sway my hips
to the music I hear,
a rhythm we create
when we make love.

SHADRESS DENISE

RAIN SHOWERS

I see you watching me.
I see how you are filled
with so much admiration
as it flows through my hair.
Your eyes speak of astonishment, as
every inch of it
gives my skin such a glow.
I turn to give you a better view,
only to see the seductive look
held hostage in your eyes.
You smile with such amazement.
Fascinated at how every drop
falls perfectly over my small brown frame.
Knowing the ways, you
view rain will never be the same.

INSANITY

I am caught up in a deep thought.
As the days go by I realize I
haven't heard your voice.
The hours have passed
by so quickly and I realize
I haven't felt your touch in months.
The memories begin to cloud my mind, as
the scent you used to wear
takes over my senses.
I lift my fingers to my
lips,
remembering the
softness of your kiss.
I close my eyes and I
see you standing
with your arms wide open,
ready for me to run to you.
I feel the tears fall
down my face like rain,
as I shake my head
trying to erase the thoughts
that have taken over my brain.

PEEP SHOW

I see you step out of your car,
and I know it's time.
I run to my window
to see what you have in
store for her tonight.
As I pull up my chair,
I see how she has already
undressed herself,
and instantly I become jealous.

I quickly strip off
my clothes as I see you walk in.
You smile when you see her,
indicating you are pleased.
You start to take off your clothes,
but she stops you
wanting to finish the
job you started. I
begin to caress my
breasts as you
start to kiss her in a way
that seems so soft.

I spread my legs apart, as I
watch you enter her. My
body begins to shake,
as my fingers create a pleasure I
can no longer control.
My body flies into a rage
as I watch her fingers dig
deep into your skin.

LIBERATED

I see you fall down by
her side as I move to
close my window.
Happy and fully satisfied
from tonight's show.

SHADRESS DENISE

SELFISH

Unable to give love,
because my heart has
been torn apart.
Unable to think about love,
because my mind
is heavy with corrupted thoughts.
Disabling my arms to welcome love,
because I am holding myself.
Constantly building barriers so
I can be protected
from the dangers love brings.
Unable to see the beauty of love,
because I am hiding behind past things.

LIBERATED

CORRUPT

Why do I do this?
Why do I self-destruct
every good thing that
comes my way?
Why do I fear love, and
enable myself the
ability to trust?
How do I manage
to intensify the very
thing that breaks me down?
How do I see the bad in
everything,
without even trying to find the good?

SHADRESS DENISE

THE PRICE OF FREEDOM

In deep goes the knife, as
I look into your eyes and
take your life.
You never treated me right,
and I have finally grown
tired of all the fights.
I can finally breakaway and be me.
No more painful nights of lockdown,
lies and abuse,
because I am finally free.

As the tears run down my face
and hit the floor, I smile at the thought of never
having to deal with anymore of your whores.
Your constant abuse that
turned my smiles into frowns,
your harsh words
that left me feeling abandoned
and emotionally broken down.
I look into the mirror
and my heart aches at how I
destroyed myself,
living in a world created by hate.

I wipe my hands and turn my back to
the person I once called my man.
I step over his body as it lays on the ground.
I opened the door without looking around,
leaving the past behind me;
with nothing to say about

LIBERATED

the world that had me so trapped,
I had to take a life to break free.

SHADRESS DENISE

POETRY TO ME

It is my vacation.
It takes me places
that reality sometimes
won't let me go.
It allows me to be
in a different
place at a different time.
It gives my emotions volume
so they can be heard.
It gives meaning
to letters that to the ordinary eye,
may just be considered words.

BAGGAGE

When there is nothing worth
fighting for and the things
that mattered before,
no longer carry a care
in the world.
When you begin to
hide because of all the
things he did to bring you
shame and the smile that
love once gave is no
longer the same.
When love is no
longer a gift,
but a burden that has
become too much to bear.
A fight you can no longer
win because your heart has given up.

ABANDONED

How can I hate you,
when I never knew
what loving you was like.
When do I learn to forgive you for
the selfish choices you made in
regards to my life.
Never willing to step
forward and give into sacrifice,
you always ran away at the
opportunity for compromise.
How am I supposed to know
how true love should be,
when the man who helped
give me life doesn't really love me.

LIBERATED

ESCAPE

Dear God,

Give me wings,
so that I can fly
far way,
to a place that
allows my soul
to breathe.

Give me a heart that
is pure and unable
to be broken from
the pain love
brings.

FORGIVENESS

As I sit and contemplate this,
I realize that opening
my heart again is a huge risk.
As anger and hatred
lie beneath the surface,
resentment reveals that
my heart is not capable of forgiveness.
Loving you was easy,
but my mind won't let me forget this. I
waited for you to change,
though you decided
things were fine.
Love continued on
and my heart decided I
wasn't a quitter.
Now two years later,
everything has grown cold
and I can no longer
fight the urge to be bitter. I
remained loyal as
I constantly fought
the thought of what I
did to deserve this.
I think about all the struggles you
put me through only
to realize I don't owe you shit.

LIBERATED

PAIN RELIEVER

He strokes my hair
relieving me of the headache
your lies have caused me.
I melt
as his hands slowly caresses
my back
giving me a comforting feeling
you once gave.
He pulls me close to listen
to a rhythm that hasn't lost its beat.
His lips on my inner thigh creating a
gratifying sensation of heat.

SHADRESS DENISE

DESIRES

It has a voice and it
screams out loud.
It fights so hard and yet, it
yearns to be held. It
gives so much and
receives so little.
It cringes at the thought of
everlasting   loneliness
and craves the sensuality
of another beat,
another sound.
It grows as it reveals
and understands its
sole purpose.
A divine rhythm that
unites to beat
and march to one drum.

LIBERATED

CONVERSATION

We laugh and talk
for what seems like hours.
You listen to me pour
my heart out and you
make me feel like
everything is going to
be okay.
I feel comfort in
you knowing my
deepest secrets and
keeping them tucked away.
You help me not fear love,
yet understand that
it is a gift that
should be embraced.
I'm in love with someone who
takes me as I am instead of
trying to make me become
something
I am not.
With you I am never
compromising my inner self.
Never giving into a love
that leads nowhere.
The sound of your voice
brings about a newness every
time I hear you speak.
An unknown feeling
that leaves me

SHADRESS DENISE
mesmerized and weak.

LIBERATED

STOLEN MOMENTS

Each time we make love, I
think about how long it
will be before I
feel your touch again.
I quiver as you carefully
place each kiss on its rightful spot.
I mentally explode at
the thought
of what you entering
me will feel like.
You give me such pleasure
as we reach the place we
so anxiously want to arrive.
Afterwards, I watch you gather
your things as I smile thinking
about how we
get lost in our stolen moments.

SHADRESS DENISE

Surreal

The sexy sounds it sings as
it captures your heart, by
way of your ear.
It leaves you on the edge
as you wait to hear the
next note it plays.
It commands your attention as
you listen
with an open ear.

You lose yourself in its song
as your mind drifts
off to a fantasy
you hope will come true.
You feel ecstasy creeping in, as
the sound serenades
your heart and calms your soul.
I move my body slowly as the
sound becomes physically
appealing to me.

I inhale slowly as
I constantly breathe in
this high that has
brought me to my feet.
Like two souls intertwined
my body stops,
as I hear the sound

LIBERATED

slowing fade away.
I exhale,
releasing the pleasure,
the sound has allowed
me to feel for that moment.

REBIRTH

A warm feeling on a cold day.
I hear a beat that silences my
lips and revives my heart. I
reach out my hand and you
pull me close.
We stare into each other eyes,
intrigued by the mystery and
curiosity that lies beneath them. The
steady rhythm of your heart
hypnotizes me as your scent sends me
on a high I never want
to come down from.
I breathe in your love
as the heat from your body ignites
a fire I thought I could no longer
burn.

LIBERATED

COLD TURKEY

I've been here before,
sedated and on the up
side of this world.
I've been lifted higher
and higher as
I constantly feed my
body the fix it needs
to keep itself alive.
The illusions
flood my mind,
as the drug flows
throughout my veins.
I move slowly as
I embrace the beauty
of this world.
I suddenly feel a
sharp pain pierce
through me as I
slowly feel this
world fading away.
My skin is itching,
as my body signals
to me its need for
its next hit.
I search for the drug,
but I realize it's all gone.
I lay here alone;
shaking, crying and

SHADRESS DENISE

in pain as the drug
wears off sending my
soul through withdrawals.

LIBERATED

UPSIDE DOWN

Day in and day out,
sun up or sun down,
She feels it coming.
There is never a warning,
it just comes.
She never feared it when you were happy,
only when you were mad.
Now it seems to appear whether
there is a smile or a frown on your face
Good or bad day,
She fears there is no way out.
She used to feel shouting would open a door,
but she soon learned the truth once you beat her,
until she could not get off the floor.
Love is a gamble;
love is a game.
It has become so harsh and unbearable.
It knows nothing, but pain.

SHADRESS DENISE

DREAM CHASER

He invades my thoughts,
as I close my eyes to fall asleep.
He knows my deepest desires
and what my body needs.
He fulfills the craves
my body screams
and shouts.
He walks through my
fantasies never wanting
to walk out.
He touches my spirit
and seizes my soul.
He stimulates my mind,
leaving me complete as
our hearts unite and
become whole.

LIBERATED

FREEDOM DANCE

When it speaks,
it speaks of you.
The sound it plays is
for the movement of
your feet alone.
The dance you do is
to the unrecognizable beat.
The intensity you have
when you move your hips,
solely reacts to the smile
upon your lips.
The curve forms in your body as
the music playing creates a
reflection of your body swaying
from side to side.
Guiding your hands to
reach out releasing the
burning, satisfying,
pleasure it inhales and exhales; as
it screams and shouts
for you to dance and be free.
The sound it makes as I
laugh out loud feeling
your control being lifted off of me.

SHADRESS DENISE

DOSAGE

It feels me up and my body
slowly becomes at ease,
as my mind travels
to a euphoric state.
The illusions cloud my thoughts and
seduces my soul
into an unknown realm.
I am in an unmarked territory as
the narcotic speeds up
the rhythm my heart now beats.
The desires have been
injected and the craves
have taken over me.
The things that were once
forbidden in my dreams have
become my reality.
I inhale deeply as the passion
fills up my soul.
I exhale giving into the drug
releasing all control.

LIBERATED

NO SUBSTITUTION

Sound off and ring the bell.
This chick thinks she can have my man,
and it's about to be some hell.
Where was she when
he was looking a mess?
Nowhere to be found,
until he learned how to dress.
No woman wanted him when
all he had was drama.
Now every gold digging tramp is
lined up around
the corner cause he
making a comma.
There were no groupies
before he changed his appearance.
Now night after night,
I'm blocking bullshit.
These chicks didn't care
and none of them were ever there.
Hustling on the streets,
raggedy clothes on his back and
dirty shoes on his feet. Now here
we are my man and me, living out
our lives,
the love we imagined in our dreams.
I can't take a deep
breath from blocking hoes
and their grimy schemes.

SHADRESS DENISE

I've sculpted, molded, and
perfected his world.
I be damned if I
give him up and
be replaced by some other girl.

LIBERATED

FIRE STARTER

My skin burns from the
anger I feel inside when I
see you with her.
Acid forms the tears that
flood my face when your
face flashes before my
eyes.

The bitterness takes over my mind
when someone mentions your name.
Igniting the jealousy
that flows throughout my veins.
Confusion clouds my mind as
the hurt I am constantly
reminded of drives me insane.
Her persuasive words are what
drew us apart.

The hatred that dwells within me,
gives life to my broken heart.
I can't explain why I am
causing self-inflicting pain, my
mind cannot comprehend why I
continue to
play this game.

My eyes are wide open,
yet everything around me is so dark.
Infidelity breathes life back into me,
creating a fire rejection
allowed me to start.

SHADRESS DENISE

UNDERESTIMATED

I placed myself into the hands of
misery and heartbreak.
I gave control to a man
that didn't have control over himself.
I trusted someone who didn't understand
the value of it.
I gave my whole heart to
this god and he treated me like shit. I
placed him on a pedestal,
constantly lifting him higher and higher.

Allowing him to reap the benefits of my love,
regardless of him being a habitual liar.
Mentally destroyed, yet I
still believed in our fate.
Slowly dying inside holding on to
a love that had no weight.
Eager to be loved, cherished,
and appreciated the way I should be.
Ready to break the chains control
and misery had over me.
Escaping a love that grew into hate.
Standing in unknown territory,
stripped and relieved to finally be free.

ACCEPTANCE

As I grab my bags, I
hear you say,
"Can we talk for a moment,
we shouldn't end it like this."

My heart is broken and
my mind is so tired of this.
So now I am leaving and we
cannot talk about shit. I
turn to face you,
as you ask the question
what did I do.

You had me fucked up
and you played me for a
damn fool.

Constantly thinking I was going to
be here each time
you left and came back. You
stand here begging, crying
out your last plea.
Fighting for me not to quit.
I kiss you goodbye.
Heartbreak was the bed
you made so lie in it.

POSSESSED

Brainwashing me into
thinking I was ugly
and no one would want me.
Locking me behind
closed doors so I
wouldn't be heard or seen.
Telling me what
you wanted me to hear,
so I would be alright.
Finding out the only time
your mouth opened
was when you told lies.
Treating me like
my heart didn't exist,
knowing damn well
love doesn't feel like this.

LIBERATED

illusions

I am his fix,
his escape from reality.
The key that unlocks
his cage when he needs to be free.
I am the person he molds
to be the woman of his dreams.
I am the thought his
mind wanders to when
she yells and screams.
I am the beat
that brings him to his feet.
I am the first call
he makes when he feels
he needs to creep.
I am the woman that unravels the
damage heartbreak has done.
I am the woman
despite what she has done;
will always remain
behind the woman who is number one.

SHADRESS DENISE

BEDTIME SECRETS

I awake as I hear
a sound that makes
my heart sink.
I focus on what he
is saying because the
thought alone has me
scared to think.
Fighting the feeling of fatigue,
I listen to the conservation
he has in his sleep.
The way he moves and
the things he is
saying makes me believe I
am not the woman
in his dreams.
He calls her name and
I realize this is no
longer a game. I
continue to listen,
shocked at the things I hear.
Wondering if I have ever
whispered the contents
of my affair in his ear.

LIBERATED

TWISTED

Confused and
not sure
about what's really going on.
Standing strong in denial as
if you did nothing wrong.
Typical of you to
say everything
I've seen and heard is not true,
completely thrown off at the fact that
you think I'm really a damn fool.
Listening to pleas for
yet another chance,
smiling letting you know how you had me
fucked up thinking I was going to continue
sharing my man.
Closing the door to our
relationship in your face,
acknowledging the fact this
heart is no longer your space.

SHADRESS DENISE

CONSUMPTION

Drawn into a world
I thought I could control.
Reaching for an invisible door,
I can't seem to open.
Ready to escape this
world of pain,
worried that this
has become my
reality and is no
longer
a game.

LIBERATED

OVERDOSE

The obsession you have
with this substance
is unexplainable.
The high you reach
cannot be easily obtained.
The rush of adrenaline your
body gives,
increases the flow of blood
throughout your veins.
It makes you see things
that may not be real.
It makes your body give
into things you yearn to feel.
Your temperature rises as
you reach the point of no return.
The pleasure begins to flow
and the substance leaks out.
I lay still trying
to kick the habit,
I know is a bitch to kick.
Gradually giving in to
the crave I know the
substance can fix.

REPLACED

Here I stand,
confused and
unsure of what to do.
Hurt and angry as I realize I
am the other woman
and now I stand in her shoes.
I figure the love I gave wasn't
good enough,
as I stare at the
boxes full of my things
he decided to pack.
I gaze at the pictures on
the walls,
as the tears
fall down my face.
Full of unsettling anger
as my thoughts
drift off into space.
Coming to grips with
falling out of love.
Fighting this feeling
of resentment
and being replaced.

LIBERATED

ARRIVED

It is a feeling that
has brought about a change.
A feeling that empowers
me and nothing else feels the same.
What is this feeling
that has released all
of my pain causing me
to scream out,
as I call its name.
How do I control the smile
it has put on my face, while
I am moving and shifting
everything in its rightful place.
A feeling that makes
me feel it can do no wrong.
Giving into a man my
soul calls home.

SCENT

It takes over me when you're near. It
pushes me pass my limitations, and
releases me from my fears.
I close my eyes to inhale you. Your
touch and your caress gives me
such erotic vibrations.
Your smile and your eyes,
such sweet temptations.
The rush you give me,
flows like air through an open vent.
The explosions of orgasms I get
when I am subdued by your scent.

LIBERATED

SEXUALLY UNLEASHED

He goes places you don't go,
and sees things you are blinded by. He
explores territories pride keeps you
from exploring.
He takes me to levels you
have never reached, and
teaches me things you
were scared to teach.
He puts his hands in
places you fear, he
makes me scream,
until I shed pleasure tears.
He shows me things
about you I've always hated, as
he opens me up,
until I'm completely released.

VACANT

She opened her eyes
and realized he was gone.
She cradled herself
to make the pain go away.
She wanted him to see what was in her eyes.
She wanted him to be true to her,
she wanted him to stop telling her lies.
She held herself tighter
as the tears ran down her face;
screaming out, knowing deep down love never
dwelled within this place.
She had insisted on making him see,
she could be all the woman he ever needed.
She felt the pain rush through her body
as she remembered how she humiliated
herself when she started begging and
pleading.
More tears ran down her face,
covering the bruises
love forced his hand to place.

LIBERATED

CLOSURE

Giving up without a fight,
knowing whatever we say
won't make it right.
The silence between us
forms a foundation
for hate to lay,
as the time has come
for us to finally break
away.
My eyes free the tears, as
I stand to
walk out the door.
Realizing this was over long ago,
admitting love, no longer resides
here anymore.

SHADRESS DENISE

LISTEN

You should have listened
when I told you I couldn't
take the pain anymore.
You should have listened
when I told you I was tired
of sleeping alone. You
should have known that it
wouldn't be long before I
ventured out
on my own.

You should have been home
each night to prevent the
tears I cried.
You should have listened to me
when I told you how I
was feeling inside.
Now you are watching me
as I begin to pick up my bags and go.
Regretting each moment, you
left me alone to be with your hoes.

LIBERATED

IDENTITY CRISIS

I look deep inside and I see me.
A woman that has come
to a fork in the road of love.
No longer allowing you to
turn me away, breaking me
down constantly day after
day.
I am standing here
not sure of where I should turn,
scared to move because of the
things I have learned.
I reach out and grab a hold
to the woman
who is no longer your fool.
The woman I was
before I knew you.

LIBERATED

Realizing
how hard it is to kick this habit.
Trying to force myself
to be strong enough to let you go.
Soul searching
to find out how I got here.
Admitting to myself
I have suppressed my feelings because
of fear.
Breaking myself down
so that I can build me back up.
Fighting the urge
to crawl back to the drug that gave me such a
rush.

LIBERATED

STRIPPED

Pusher is what I used to call him.
The man who introduced me to a drug I never
thought I would become addicted to.
He would constantly feed my body a narcotic it
finally became dependent upon.
Constantly down and heartbroken when he was
around,
never know how long my mind
would be wandering in the lost and found.

Suffering from withdrawals, not
sure when he would return;
I found a new love in a man named Shooter.
He would take my body to orgasmic levels you
could never comprehend.
He shared what I thought was ours with others.
Easily misusing the gifts, I thought he should
treasure.
Uncertain of what would happen if I
walked out of misery's door,
I remained faithful to this man allowing myself to
be treated like a whore.

Consumed by fear and blinded by a drug
I couldn't see;
I gave into being weak and fell onto another
man's feet.
Abused and strung out with nothing left to give,
I gave it all to him.
Every burden and every problem I could no longer hold.

SHADRESS DENISE

Freeing myself from every spirit,
I collected and held hostage within my soul.

LIBERATED

TRICKED

Cold, shaking
and constantly blacking out;
I finally open my eyes
to see the walls closing in on me. I
turn to see you walking away and I
begin to breakdown.

Unstable
and not in my right state of mind,
you watch me lose control.
I try to fight this feeling
that has turned me out,
moving to find what I know
will bring you back.

Injecting myself
with the chaotic pleasure
you once adored.
The drug that took over my mind,
allowing me to be your beautiful
version of a Madonna whore.

TURNED OUT

I exhale as I once again allow you to slide it in.
I feel the heat rush through my body
as your remedy of choice reaches my heart.
My eyes become heavy as the fix
I have been craving takes over my mind.
My body is numb and my adrenaline
is pumping as you continue to inject me with
a substance that makes me drift off to a euphoric
state.
I lie still realizing I have become an
overworked addict;
believing lust became love and what we have is
fate.

LIBERATED

RECOVERED

I lay here toes
curled, knees
buckled,
and my ankles shackled to a
love that I lived for.
Addicted to a man
that constantly drew me
deeper into his world.
My soul cried out
and I needed to be free.
Released from this spirit
that took over me, binding
and controlling
a mind that needed to breathe.
Unleashed,
yet possessed.
Subdued,
but somehow freed
from this feeling I
feel when this narcotic is
injected to control and
overpower me.

THE LAST TIME

As I stand embraced in your arms,
I realize how I must cherish this moment.
As I inhale your scent,
I remember the long nights we spent
creating many sweet aromas.
The sound of your heartbeat makes
mine flutter once again.
I pull you closer trying to
orchestrate the harmony our
rhythms once shared.
I feel a teardrop fall
and I smile at how much love
we once held inside;
acknowledging that love
has to once again say goodbye.

LIBERATED

JUDGMENT

Standing still, waiting
for it to come. Ready to
turn around,
knowing it will eventually find me.
Resisting the urge to fight, understanding
this was destined to be.

SHADRESS DENISE

DEATH SENTENCE

To keep the man, I loved,
I chose wrong over right.
Presented with yet another chance, I
accepted darkness over light.
I placed another life in his hands,
knowing I would
eventually pay the price.
I walked beside the devil,
afraid to leave his world.
Willing to sacrifice the life of my
unborn child,
all in the name of being his girl.

LOVE'S FATALITY

As I stand here ready
to end it all, I
realize how much
more life I could
have seen if you had
not broken my heart. I
realize how long
I have been addicted
to you and I no longer want
to feel the way I feel.
Constantly going through
withdrawals because you're
not here.
Willing to remain
strung out because losing
you is my biggest fear.
Distraught with
the idea of being alone, I
swallow my peace, knowing
hell will now be my new
home.

SHADRESS DENISE

DEVIL'S KITCHEN

Here I sit.
Ready to share another day,
another moment in time with
this man I call love.
Constantly eating at the table,
feeding myself nothing but misery.
Full of regret,
denial and pain.
Throwing up all of the
nutrients I need to
remain sane.
Fighting a battle,
I know I can't win;
while setting the table
to eat another meal,
I know will leave me empty within.

LIBERATED

SET UP

Plotted and schemed,
because you were the man of my dreams.
I told you things to let you think
what I wanted you to think.
Acting out so many mischievous things,
until the lines turned pink.
Repeatedly playing a dangerous
game with two souls,
selfishly thinking of myself
and misusing birth control.
Lying and playing so many tricks, to
get a piece of dick.
Physically breaking down,
admitting to myself I am sick.

HEALING

Your voice brings about a
stillness that frees
my spirit and soothes my soul.
No longer able to
carry the heavy burdens, I
lay them at your feet.
As the tears
flow down my face,
you hold out your hand.
Leading me away from
the pain that was once
my dwelling place.

LIBERATED

CIVILIZED EVIL

A cold state, but a warm touch.
Unable to feel the rhythm of your heart;
I move closer,
only to hear a different beat.
Realizing that we are no longer one,
I rest my head on your chest.
Listening to the sound that is
now her song.

SHADRESS DENISE

BLIND SENSES

Colorful stories that
clouded my judgment,
while shutting down my
senses.
Unreal statements
that seduced my
thoughts and made me
give everything to you.

LIBERATED

CONFESSIONS

I am standing here
with the things I
can no longer bare.
My hands are heavy
and my mind is
full of things I never
thought I would share.
Abortions, abuse and
drugs are the demons
that dwell within my soul.
An irate love I could
no longer control.
Foolish to think
withdrawal would be
a natural feeling.
Wanting to move on, but
unable to reach out and
receive my healing.

SILENCED PLEA

Screaming out,
but unable to be heard.
Reaching
for something that's not even there.
Carrying a burden
that's not even mine.
While my skin is burning
from this unfamiliar drug.
I am lonely and crying out
inside
from something that feels like love.

IMPERFECTIONS

I reach over to shoot up with what I
feel will make them go away.
As my mask races throughout my body, I
accept I no longer know who I am.
Each night, I roll over to hold a man who
treats me as if I don't exist.
Punching, laughing and mistreating me
by calling me his bitch.
I place it on the table
as the last drop flows down my throat.
Seeing my reflection in this
bottle,
realizing there is no
hope.

BRICK WALL

I possess heavy hands
and a broken heart
from the things I have received.
I can't see them,
but I know they are there.
Every time I make a move forward, I
feel them pull me back.
The constant reminders of what we had;
the love that no longer
dwells in my heart.
The trust that is no more
because of all the women
you fucked in our bed,
each time you opened this door.
The tears are warm and fast
as they race down my face. The
pain eases up as I begin to
move further
from this place.
I watch you kneel and fall,
screaming out as I step over you.
I smile one last time,
speechless with nothing left to say;
leaving the past behind this wall.

Hailing from St. Louis, MO, Shadress Denise is an author, graphic designer, and journalist. She has been writing poetry and short stories for over 10 years. She has published two books of poetry and two novels. *Disturbia* and *Hello. Goodbye. Never Again*; collections of poetry. *Who Do You Love & Who Do You Love Too?* Erotic fiction novels.

Shadress has earned her Bachelors of Science in Graphic Design and a Masters of Art in Communications. As the She is a journalist for The Urban Release, a writer for DELUX magazine, and the owner of ColorMeBlu Designs. Shadress continues to build her brand through writing and graphic design. Still residing in her hometown, she is currently preparing to release the final part of her book series Who Do You Love (Who Do You Love Now?) and other upcoming projects.

SHADRESS DENISE

MORE TITLES BY SHADRESS DENISE

www.iamshadressdenise.com

www.ingramcontent.com/pod-product-compliance
Lightning Source LLC
Chambersburg PA
CBHW061449040426
42450CB00007B/1277